Get set... GO!
Painting

Ruth Thomson

Contents

CHILDRENS PRESS®
CHICAGO

Getting ready

This book shows you lots of ways
to experiment with paint.
The best paints to use are water-based paints:

*Powder paint must be mixed
with water to make it creamy.*

*Tempera blocks are solid.
You must dampen them before use.*

*Acrylic paint is thick
and creamy. It comes in tubes.
It can be thinned with water.*

Poster paints can be thinned with water.

Finger paint is very thick.

Buy red, yellow, blue, black, and white paints.
Mix them to make other colors.
Before you begin, cover your table with
newspaper and put on an old shirt or a smock.

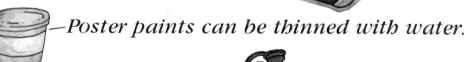

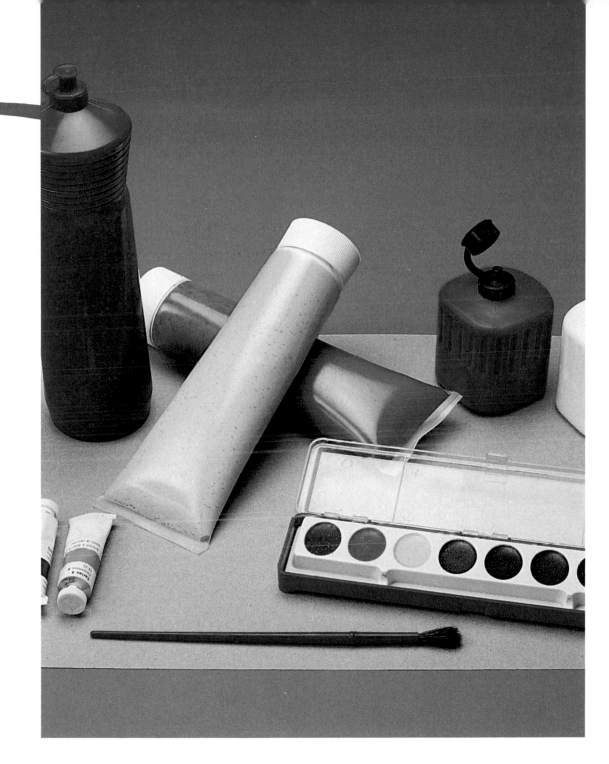

Color combing

Get ready

- ✔ Cardboard
- ✔ Safety scissors
- ✔ Finger paint
- ✔ Tray
- ✔ Paper

. . . Get Set

Cut a rectangle of cardboard
about the size of your hand.
Cut notches along one edge
to make your comb.
Spread finger paint all over the tray.

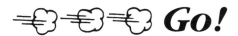 **Go!**

Draw patterns in the paint
with your comb.
Put a sheet of paper
on the wet paint.
Smooth it down lightly.
Lift it off to see your print.

5

Painting with wood

Get ready

✔ Spoon   ✔ Paper   ✔ Small piece
✔ Thick paint   ✔ Cardboard   of wood

. . . Get Set

Put two spoonfuls of paint
on a sheet of paper.
Spread the paint evenly over the
paper with the edge of the cardboard.

 Go!

While the paint is still wet,
draw a picture in it
with the end of the wood.
Try other materials,
such as a feather and a cork.

Dot pictures

Get ready

- ✔ Pencil
- ✔ Paper
- ✔ Straws

- ✔ Palette or old saucers

- ✔ Thick paints

. . . Get Set

Draw a picture or a pattern lightly in pencil on the paper. Squeeze paints onto a palette— or use saucers, one for each color.

 **Go!**

Dip the tips of the straws into the paints.
Color your picture.
Use one straw for each color.

Bubble patterns

Get ready

- ✔ Dishwashing liquid
- ✔ Small container
- ✔ Teaspoon
- ✔ Paint
- ✔ A straw

. . . Get Set

Squeeze some dishwashing liquid into the container.
Add a teaspoon of paint and stir well.

Go!

Blow gently into the mixture through the straw.
Keep blowing until bubbles rise
over the edge of the container.
Lay some paper over the bubbles.
The pattern will transfer onto the paper.
Cover the whole sheet of paper like this.

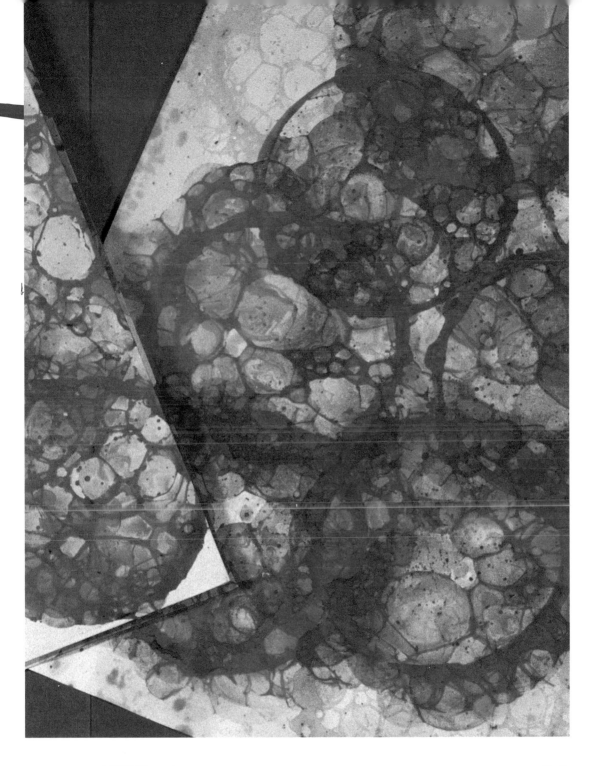

Marbling

Get ready

✔ Flat-bottomed pan filled with cold water

✔ Marbling colors
✔ Straws
✔ Paper

. . . Get Set

Use the straws to drip spots of marbling colors onto the water. Use a separate straw for each color.

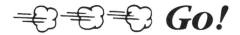 ## Go!

Stir the water gently to spread the color.
Drop some paper onto the water.
Let it float for a moment.
Take the paper out and let it dry.
Use your marbled paper as wrapping paper or as a background for a picture.

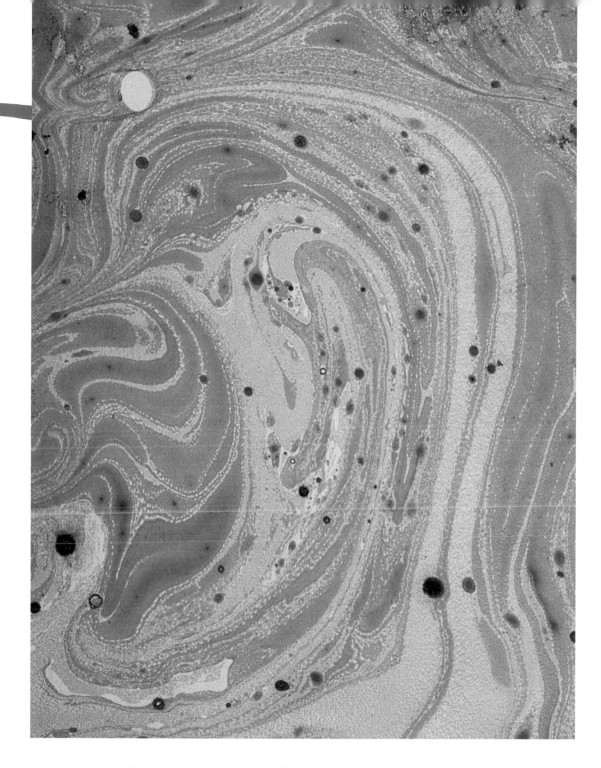

Marbled paper collage

Get ready

✔ Several sheets of marbled paper

✔ Safety scissors
✔ Glue

✔ Construction paper

. . . Get Set

Make some sheets of marbled paper in contrasting colors. (See page 12.)

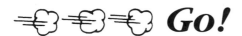 **Go!**

Cut the paper into shapes, such as hills, mountains, trees, waves, and houses. Glue them on the construction paper to make a picture.

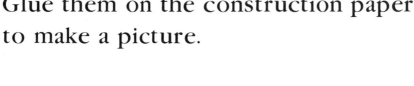

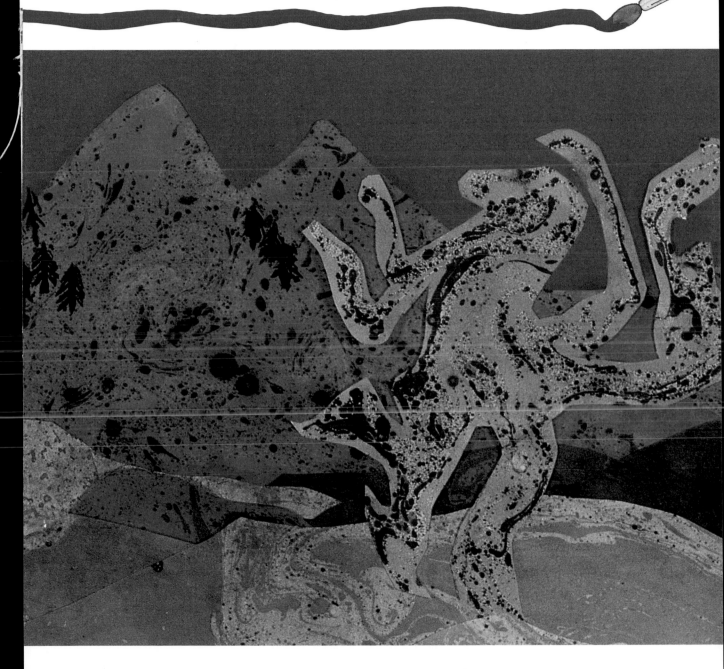

Magic painting

Get ready

- ✔ Water-based paint
- ✔ Paintbrush
- ✔ Paper
- ✔ India ink
- ✔ Pan of water

. . . Get Set

Paint a picture in lines using only one color. Let it dry.

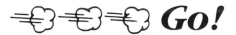 Go!

Gently brush India ink over the painting and let it dry. Soak the painting in water. Rub it with your fingers. The paint will dissolve, but the ink is waterproof.

Acrylic painting

Get ready

- ✔ Powder paints
- ✔ Small containers
- ✔ Tablespoon
- ✔ Acrylic paint
- ✔ Palette
- ✔ Palette knife
- ✔ Construction paper or thin cardboard

. . . Get Set

Put a heaping tablespoon of
powder paint into a container.
Slowly add water and stir
until the paint is creamy.
Add acrylic paint until the mixture
is stiff and hard to stir.

✿✿✿ *Go!*

Tip some paint onto a palette.
Use the palette knife to paint a picture
on some heavy paper or thin cardboard.

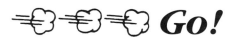

Splatter and drip

Get ready

- ✔ Newspaper
- ✔ Tubes of paint
- ✔ Table knife
- ✔ Construction paper
- ✔ Paintbrush
- ✔ Old toothbrush

. . . Get Set

This kind of painting is very messy.
Cover the floor and table with newspaper.
Put on an old shirt or a smock.

Go!

Squeeze paint from
the tubes onto the paper.
Make squiggles and whorls.
Squeeze paint onto the toothbrush
and flick with the table knife to get fine drips.
Splatter drops of paint with the paintbrush.

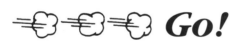

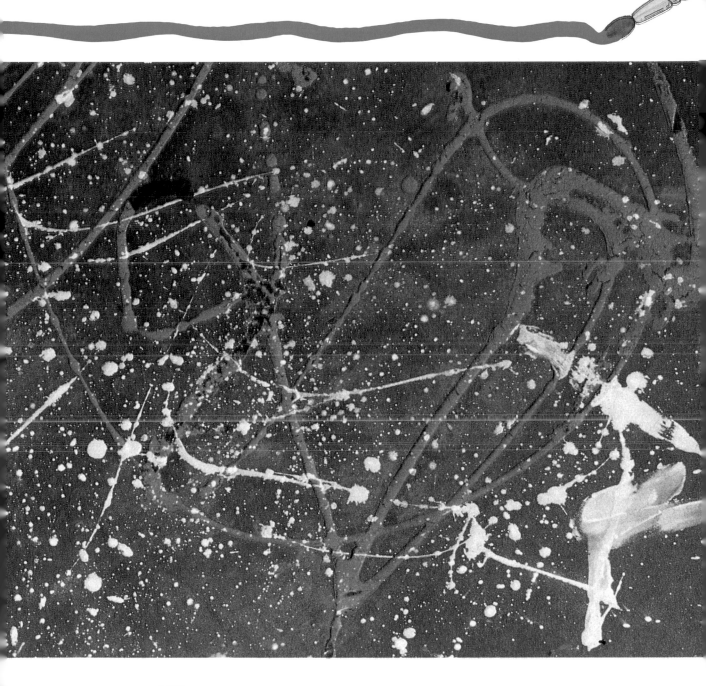

Painting with a roller

Get ready

- ✔ Plastic tray
- ✔ Thick paints
- ✔ Paint roller
- ✔ Paintbrush
- ✔ Construction paper

. . . Get Set

Squeeze some paint onto the tray.
Coat the roller with paint.
Roll it back and forth across the paper.
Roll more than one color
for a rich effect.
Let the paint dry.

⇒⇒⇒ Go!

Paint a picture on top
of your textured background.

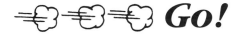

Index

Photographic credits: Pp. 9, 19: John Butcher (artwork supplied by Henry Pluckrose); Pp. 3, 5, 7, 11, 13, 15, 17: Chris Fairclough Colour Library (artwork supplied by Henry Pluckrose); Pp. 21, 23: Henry Pluckrose

Editor: Pippa Pollard
Design: Jane Felstead
Cover design: Mike Davis
Artwork: Jane Felstead

Library of Congress Cataloging-in-Publication Data

Thomson, Ruth.
    Painting / by Ruth Thomson.
        p.   cm. — (Get set— go!)
    Includes index.
    ISBN 0-516-07990-5
    1. Painting—Technique—Juvenile literature. [1. Painting—Technique.] I. Title. II. Series.
    ND1500.T525   1994
    751.4—dc20   94-16938
                                                             CIP
                                                              AC

1994 Childrens Press® Edition
© 1993 Watts Books, London, New York, Sydney
All rights reserved. Printed in the United States of America.
Published simultaneously in Canada.
1 2 3 4 5 6 7 8 9 0 R 03 02 01 00 99 98 97 96 95 94